HOORAY for DOGS

HOORAY

for DOGS

by Alexandra Day

LAUGHING ELEPHANT · MMVIII

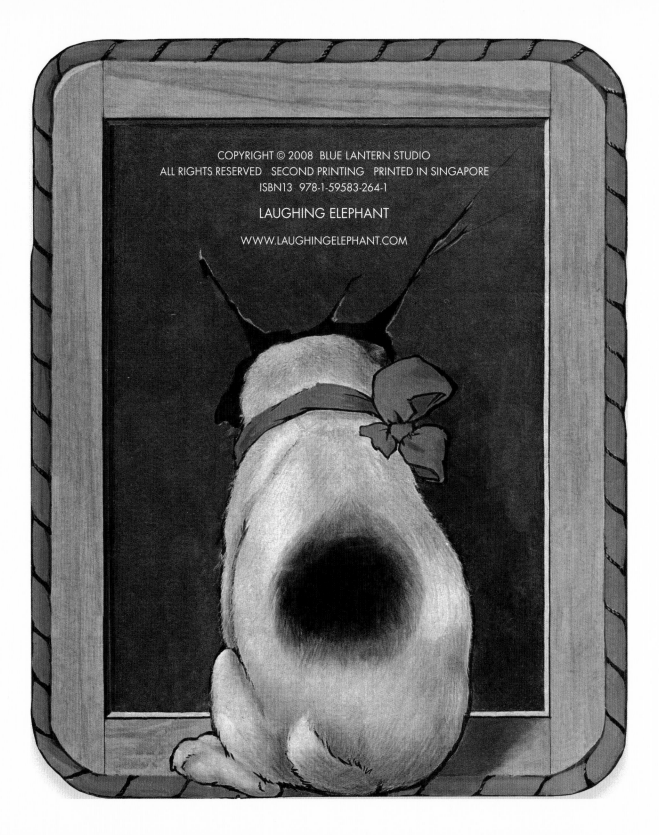

LAUGHING ELEPHANT

WWW.LAUGHINGELEPHANT.COM

Here's to our wonderful friends

I raise my glass to all Good Dogs.
To no particular breed, no special strain
Of certified prize-winners—just to plain,
Unpedigreed Good Dogs …
I drink to wagging tails and honest eyes,
To courage, and unguessed-at loyalties
Whose value never will be known or sung.

UNKNOWN

Who give us so much
LAUGHTER

It is fatal to let any dog know that he is funny, for he immediately loses his head and starts hamming it up. As an instance of this I would point to Rudolph, a dachshund I once owned, whose slogan was anything for a Laugh. Dachshunds are always the worst offenders in this respect because of their peculiar shape. It is only natural that when a dog finds that his mere appearance makes the viewing public giggle, he should assume that Nature intended him for a comedian's role.

P.G. WODEHOUSE

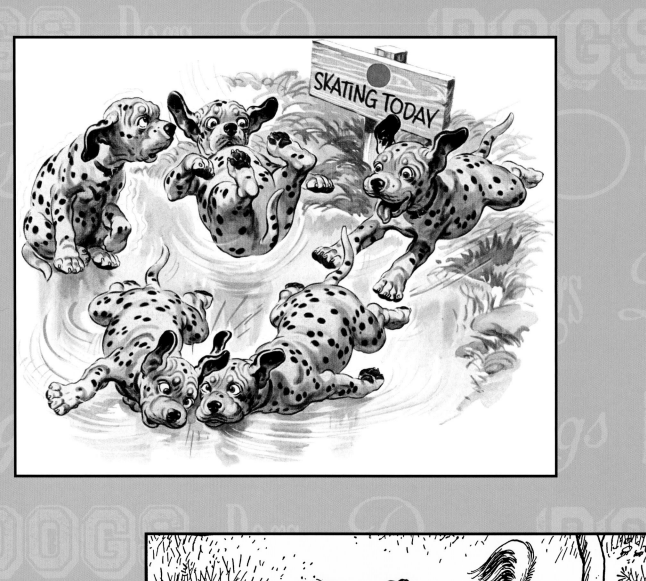

The great pleasure of a dog is that you may make a fool of yourself with him, and not only will he not scold you, but he will make a fool of himself too.

SAMUEL BUTLER

Who are always ready to provide
COMFORT & COMPANIONSHIP

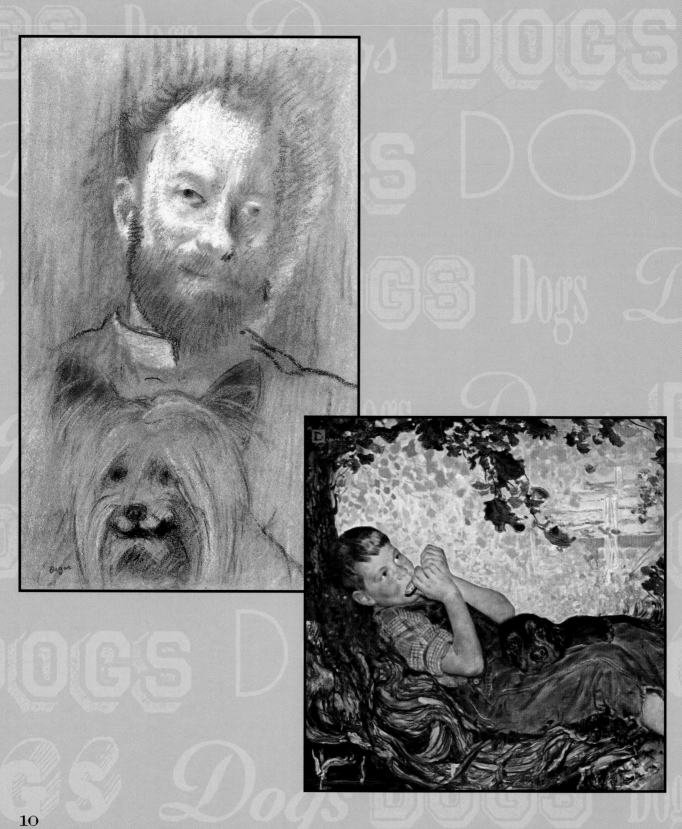

COMFORT & COMPANIONSHIP

I firmly believe that some dogs can read minds. Dixie, my Labrador, usually joins me at breakfast, and I usually give her a scrap of toast or bacon. I have often noticed that when I decide to choose a scrap for her, and well before I pick it up, she will trot to my side and stand, waiting. She must have read my mind. There's no other plausible explanation.

J. BRYAN

For the great true heart that is in his eyes,
Tender, and patient, and brave, and wise,
That makes him know when I'm sick, or sad,
And, knowing, love me the more—dear lad—
With a love unquestioning, high and fine—
For all of that Little Brown Dog of mine,
I thank thee.

ANONYMOUS

COMFORT & COMPANIONSHIP

If you eliminate smoking and gambling, you will be amazed to find that almost all an Englishman's pleasures can be, and mostly are, shared by his dog.

GEORGE BERNARD SHAW

Of all the animals, surely the dog is the only one that really shares our life, helps in our work, and has a place in our recreation. It is the only one that becomes so fond of us that sometimes it cannot go on living after its master dies.

FERMAND MERCY

COMFORT & COMPANIONSHIP

To be without a dog is worse than being without a song.

HENRY BEETLE HOUGH

Who cause such Entertaining
TROUBLE

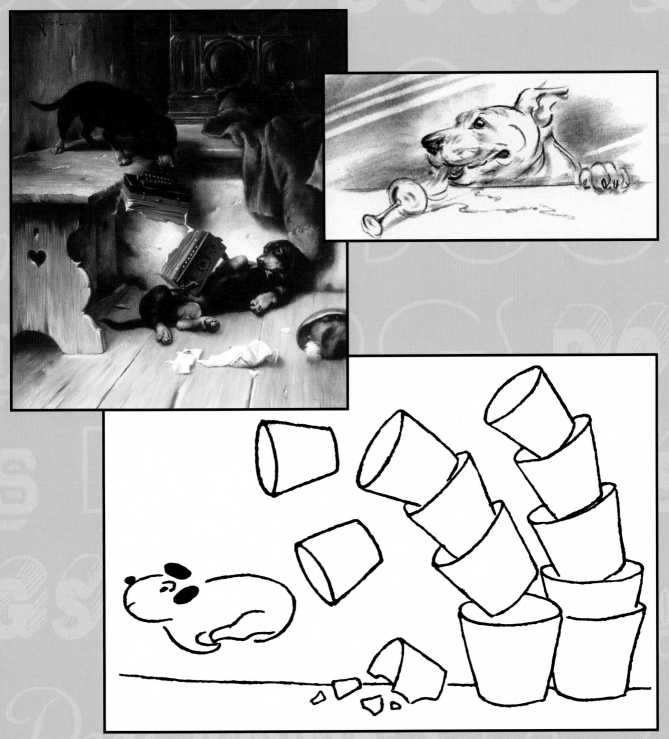

TROUBLE

When I got here
Your dogs had opened the fridge.
They took out tomatoes and a lemon.
That is all I saw.
I washed the tomatoes and put them back.

THISBE NISSEN, FOUND POEM, 1983

My home is a haven for one who enjoys
The clamor of children and ear-splitting noise
From a number of dogs who are always about,
And who want to come in and, once in, to go out.
Whenever I settle to read by the fire,
Some dog will develop an urge to retire,
And I'm constantly opening and shutting the door
For a dog to depart or as mentioned before,
For a dog to arrive, who, politely admitted,
Will make a bee-line for the chair I've just quitted.
Our friends may be dumb, but my house is a riot,
Where I can sit still and can never be quiet.

RALPH WITHERSPOON

Whose
CARE
rewards us so richly

Every dog should have a man of his own. There is nothing like a well-behaved person around the house to spread the dog's blanket for him, or bring him his supper when he comes home man-tired at night.

COREY FORD

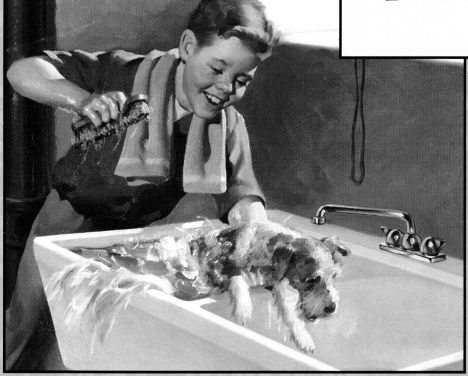

Anxious Moments

Lord Rosebery, Prime Minister of England was crossing the Irish Sea on a steamer when his dog fell overboard. The officers refused to stop the ship. Very well, said the noble lord.
If you won't stop for a dog, you'll stop for a man. And with that he took a header over the side, and both dog and man were rescued.

Their trusting
LOVE & LOYALTY
is a great example

LOVE & LOYALTY

Histories are more full of examples of fidelity of dogs than of friends.

ALEXANDER POPE

Long-distance trailing by dogs has been the subject of many legendary accounts. A Greyhound named Cesar is said to have followed his master from Switzerland to the court of Henry III in Paris. He arrived months after his owner traveled there by coach. 'Prince' in 1915 found his way across the English Channel to his master in Paris. A Parade magazine account, dated April 20, 1991, relates the odyssey of Fido, a Belgian sheepdog that spent two years crossing Europe to find his owners, Jose Redondo and Lise Dermeir, who had moved to Gijon, Spain. Lise almost stumbled over their former pet in the doorway of their new home. Fido was welcomed to stay.

MORTIMER B. ZUCKERMAN

The dog does not live that would refuse to forsake his dinner for the companionship of his master.

HENRY C. MERWIN

The hen fell to scratching, and fluffy chicks darted hither and thither, picking up the tidbits which the mother uncovered. 'Good!' said Don to himself; 'I can help in this business,' and, to the terror of the chickens, he ran among them and began turning up the soil at a lively rate. Then he sat down and waited. The mother hen called back the chicks to the newly scratched earth, and soon they picked it clean. Then the dog took another turn, and so the good work proceeded, to the great delight of all the parties.

The greatest love is a mother's; then comes a dog's; then comes a sweetheart's.

POLISH PROVERB

LOVE & LOYALTY

The kind of love a dog gives is one that does care who you are or what you are doing— if you are good tempered or bad tempered he cares about you just the same— you do not often get that from human beings. You have to take a little trouble to give something in return. But once a dog knows you are his master or mistress he cares exactly the same, no matter what you are. It is almost a divine quality— the love that nothing can alter.

MARJORIE BOWEN

The truth I do not stretch or shove
When I state the dog is full of love.
I've also proved by actual test,
A wet dog is the lovingest.

OGDEN NASH

Nobody can fully understand the meaning of love unless he's owned a dog. He can show you more honest affection with a flick of his tail than a man can gather through a lifetime of handshakes. I can't think of anything that brings me closer to tears than when my old dog— completely exhausted after a full and hard day in the field— limps away from her nice spot in front of the fire and comes over to where I'm sitting and puts her head in my lap, a paw over my knee and closes her eyes and goes to sleep. I don't know what I've done to deserve that kind of friend.

GENE HILL

You think dogs will not be in heaven? I tell you, they will be there long before any of us.

ROBERT LOUIS STEVENSON

I can still see my first dog in all moods and situations that memory has filed him away in; for six years he met me at the same place after school and convoyed me home– a service he thought up himself. A boy doesn't forget that sort of association.

E.B. WHITE

They help us with cheerful
WILLINGNESS

WILLINGNESS

The first Seeing Eye dog was a German shepherd bitch named Buddy, bred in Switzerland by Dorothy Eustis for police and rescue work. In 1928 Eustis invited a blind man from Tennessee named Morris Frank to Switzerland to work with one of her dogs. Frank and Buddy learned to work together during a five-week training period. On one occasion she dragged him away from a pair of runaway horses. When, at the end of the training period, they went to the village alone so Frank could get a haircut, he was jubilant at the simple act of independence. Frank and Buddy returned to the United States and toured the country on behalf of Seeing Eye, Inc., which was founded in 1929.

Buddy occasionally helped herself to hors d'oeuvres at receptions and acknowledged applause by barking at the audience. During her years with Frank, Buddy saved him from a hotel fire and an open elevator shaft, and she once towed him to shore when he tired during a swim.

The story of Barry, the St. Bernard dog who lived with the monks in the Convent of St. Bernard, is well known. He served the hospital in the Alps for twelve years, and saved no less than forty persons. He used to go out alone in the deep snow in search of lost travelers, barking at the top of his lungs as he went, sometimes falling from exhaustion. When he could not drag back a traveler alone, he hastened to the hospital to get assistance.

A bloodhound named Nick Carter was probably the all-time world's champion tracking dog. He was directly responsible for over 700 arrests during his career as a tracker for the Lexington, Kentucky, Police Department.

A German Shepherd named Tommy was the World War I mascot of a Scottish regiment and always went over the top with his men. He was wounded three times, was gassed when his custom-made gas mask was not put on him in time, was captured, and eventually received the Croix de Guerre for gallantry.

Over the past fifty years in the United States there have been hundreds of newspaper accounts of canine heroism, including a bulldog killed while saving a boy being attacked by three Great Danes, a Labrador retriever who protected two small girls from an attack by a rabid raccoon, an Irish setter who braved flames to rescue a little girl from a burning car, an Airedale who ran seven miles home to get help for its wounded master, and a mutt who bit a man to keep him from entering a house filled with propane gas.

During the siege of Verdun, a small detachment of French troops was cut off from its main force. Short of ammunition and zeroed-in by German artillery, they were on the verge of surrender when Satan, a collie-greyhound mix, was dispatched to the unit carrying two carrier pigeons and a message that reinforcements were on the way.

In gas mask and goggles, Satan braved intense fire to reach the besieged detachment. He was hit by a bullet but kept going on three legs. He finally reached the French soldiers, and they released the pigeons carrying the co-ordinates of the German gun position. The pigeons flew back to headquarters, French artillery knocked out the German gun, and the troops were rescued.

Their
APPRECIATION
of little things is wonderful

Puli, my dog (he is a puli and his name is Puli and it wasn't my idea), is so wonderful. In the eleven years we have had him we have always called him to dinner in the same way (briefly- 'dinner, Puli') and yet every day he turns his head in sheer wonderment and happiness for a few moments before dashing to it, not quite believing that he is really getting dinner again tonight. He may be a dog, but don't tell me he doesn't have a real grip on life.

KENDALL HAILEY

The brilliant smell of water,
The brave smell of a stone,
The smell of dew and thunder,
The old bones buried under…

The wind from winter forests,
The scent of scentless flowers,
The breath of bride's adorning,
The smell of snare and warning,
The smell of Sunday morning,
God gave to us for ours.

FROM *THE SONG OF QUOODLE* BY G. K. CHESTERTON

They live in the
MOMENT

MOMENT

I did my usual bedtime ritual of walking in a tight circle around my bed until I found just exactly the spot I wanted, and then I flopped down. Oh, that felt good!
I wiggled around and finally came to rest with all four paws sticking up in the air.
I closed my eyes and had some wonderful twitching dreams about…don't recall exactly the subject matter, but most likely they were about Beulah, the neighbor's collie. I dream about her a lot.

FROM *HANK THE COW DOG* AS TOLD TO JOHN ERICKSON

He was the biggest fool-pup I ever saw, chock full of life and spirits, always going at racing speed, generally into mischief, breaking his heart if his master did not notice him, chewing up clothing, digging up garden stuff, going direct from a wallow in the pigsty to frolic in the baby's cradle, getting kicked in the ribs by horses and tossed by cows, but still the same hilarious, rollicking, good natured, energetic fool-pup, and given by common consent the fit name of Silly Billy.

FROM *THE MAKING OF SILLY BILLY*
BY ERNEST THOMPSON SETON

Vernon Thomas

They encourage us to be
HAPPY

HAPPY

Labradors make lousy watchdogs. They usually bark when there is a stranger about, but it is an expression of unmitigated joy at the chance to meet somebody new, not a warning.

NORMAN STRUNG

The dog was created especially for children. He is the god of frolic.

HENRY WARD BEECHER

You didn't have to throw a stick in the water to get him to go in. Of course, he would bring back a stick if you did throw one in. He would even have brought back a piano if you had thrown one in.

FROM *SNAPSHOT OF A DOG*
BY JAMES THURBER

They inspire us to be
HOPEFUL

And what is the proper spirit? Chunkie's, I think, keeping one's end up, and the flag of one's tail briskly flying to the last. Wise and sensible dog; making the most of what he has, rather than worrying over what he hasn't. And ruminating on the rocks during those afternoons by the sea, it occurred to me that it would be very shameful if I were less sensible, less wholesome, and less sturdy of refusal to go down before blows, than Chunkie.

And on my hand, like sun warmed rose-leaves flung,
The least faint flicker of the warmest tongue,
And so my dog and I have met and sworn,
Fresh love and fealty for another morn.

HARDWICK DRUMMOND RAWNSLEY

HOPEFUL

There may be a bone on the kitchen floor,
There may be a cat at the scullery door,
And may be William has seen a rat,
But, thanks! I shall stay on the hall front mat.
Oh, it is silly the way each one pretends,
That he cannot think why I won't budge, my friends,
You're clever, the lot of you, but I know,
The car's coming round- and I MEAN TO GO.

FROM *NO, YOU DON'T!*
AS TOLD TO JOE WALKER

They remind us of
WONDER

Dogs, being creatures of habit and routine, find oddities the cause for riveting, often comic, attention.

HENRY C. MERWIN

Dogs, like men, are born with enormous curiosity.

HORACE WALPOLE

PICTURE CREDITS

Cover	Frank Adams. From *The Beautiful Book of Nursery Rhymes Stories and Pictures,* c. 1930.
Endpapers	Edwin Noble. From *The Dog Lover's Book,* 1910.
Frontispiece	Cecil Aldin. From *Pickles,* 1909.
Title Page	A.E. Kennedy. From *My Puppy Dog,* 1917.
Copyright	A.E. Kennedy. From *My Puppy Dog,* 1917.
1	Unknown. Greeting card, n.d.
2	Edwin Georgi. Magazine cover, 1931.
3	H.T. Webster. From *Life With Rover,* 1949.
4	(upper) Unknown. Magazine illustration, n.d., (lower) H.T. Webster. From *Life With Rover,* 1949.
5	(upper) Mrs. Ernest Ames. From *The Bedtime Book,* 1901.
	(lower) Mrs. Ernest Ames. From *Watty: A White Puppy,* c. 1910.
6	(upper) Unknown. Book illustration, n.d., (lower) Cecil Aldin. From *Mac,* 1912.
7	(upper) Cecil Aldin. From *Gyp's Hour of Bliss,* c. 1925, (lower) Unknown. Calendar, 1936.
8	Briton Rivière. "Sympathy," 1877.
9	(left) Cecil Aldin. From *Our Friend the Dog,* 1913., (right) John Hassall. Caricature, n.d.
10	(upper) Edgar Degas. "Ludovic Lepic Holding His Dog," c. 1888.
	(lower) Douglass Crockwell, c. 1946.
11	(upper) Briton Rivière. "Fidelity," 1869., (lower) Annie Benson Müller. "A Country Gentleman," 1937.
12	(upper) Percy Harland Fisher. "Her Favorite Pet," n.d., (lower) Ed Gordon. Magazine illustration, c. 1950
13	Theodore Robinson. "The Girl With The Dog," n.d.
14	Unknown. Illustration, n.d.
15	(upper) Lawrence L. Wilbur. "A Girl's Best Friend," c. 1925., (lower) Will Houghton. Poster design, n.d.
16	Cecil Aldin. From *The Cat and Dog Book,* c. 1920.
17	(upper left) Carl Reichert. "The Tug of War," 1900., (upper right) Diana Thorne. From *Diana Thorne's Dogs,* 1944.,
	(lower) Karel Capek. From *Dashenka,* 1935.
18	(upper) Cecil Aldin. From *The Merry Puppy Book,* 1913., (lower) Albert Staehle. Magazine illustration,
19	(B&W) A.B. Frost. From *Carlo,* 1913., (color) Cecil Aldin. From *Rough and Tumble,* 1919.
20	(upper) William Henry Hamilton Trood. "Uncorking the Bottle and a Surprising Result," 1887.
	(lower) H.T. Webster. From *Life With Rover,* 1949.
21	Cecil Aldin. From *Gyp's Hour of Bliss,* c. 1925.
22	Charles Burton Barber. "Not Too Much Wrong," n.d.
23	(upper) H.T. Webster. From *Life With Rover,* 1949., (lower) Charles R. Showalter. Untitled illustration, c. 1950.
24	(upper) Marguerite Davis. From *Wiggles: A Funny Little Dog,* 1936., (lower) Frances Tipton Hunter. Advertisement, 1931.
25	(upper) Unknown. "Anxious Moments," n.d., (lower) Gaston Phébus. From *Livre de Chasse,* 15th century.
26	Edwin Landseer. "Attachment," 1829.
27	Alexandra Day. From *Carl's Afternoon in the Park,* Farrar Straus & Giroux, 1991.
28	(upper) Eugen Felix. "Guarding the Baby," n.d., (lower) Unknown. Illustration, n.d.
29	(upper) Unknown. Illustration, n.d., (lower) Unknown. Calendar, 1934.
30	(upper) Arthur J. Elsley. "I'se Biggest" (1892), (lower) Briton Rivière. "Requiescat," 1889.
31	(upper) Walter Hunt Jr. "Motherless – The Shepherd's Pet," 1897., (lower) Hy Hintermeister. "Quick Pick-Up," c. 1950.
32	Edwin Noble. From *The Dog Lover's Book,* 1910.
33	(upper) Edward Herbert Miner. Painting, c. 1940., (lower) Henriette Ronner-Knip. "The Road to School," n.d.
34	(upper) Will Rannells. Magazine illustration, 1915., (center) Unknown. Advertisement, n.d.
	(lower) Lea Norris. From *Jimmy Shoestring,* 1932.

PICTURE CREDITS